Getting out of unemployment in less than 1 month

Content

The first thing to consider when looking for a job 5

What you should keep in mind about your professional profile 9

Key actions to find a job 13

Recommendations for starting a job search 16

The ideal job search plan 22

How to apply by means of a self-candidature 31

Self-employment 33

Searching for a job on the Internet 35

How to leverage the use of LinkedIn to search for jobs 67

Tips for finding a job 71

Finding a job abroad without suffering in the process 75

Find a job in digital marketing 80

Finding a job without experience 85

The best job portals 89

Tips for finding a job when you are over 50 years old 92

Guide on how to find a job

A personal goal for anyone is to achieve job stability, it works as an important livelihood for the present and future, so finding an ideal job is a key step in life, you may have other additional reasons such as unemployment, tiredness about your current situation or search for financial growth.

Regardless of the reason, you must learn how to stand out among the other applicants for a job position and get an opportunity, also so that it does not become an impossible challenge for you, you need to follow each of the recommendations set out for you to be an ideal candidate that every job offer requires.

The first thing to consider when looking for a job

When trying to look for a job and not getting positive answers, it means that you cannot overlook some factors and details when applying about a job alternative, until you get to the job opportunity you want, to accelerate this result you can consider tips that will serve as an impulse, such as the following:

- **Know yourself**

A first step to get the job of your dreams is to perform a self-assessment, as this allows you to recognize your strengths, as well as to detect the aspects in which you should work to develop or improve, by taking this into account you can aspire to have a better job presentation.

When you begin to strive to increase your capabilities, you will receive better treatment or attention for your talents, being an important boost in the selection process for being a better candidate for that job, and at the same time it works to discover the job compatible with your qualities.

Having clear your skills and aptitudes help you visualize the type of environment that fits with it, this is the answer to choose the trade or profession you want, additionally you can make a list of the goals you want to achieve at work, then you can think of tools and techniques to achieve it.

As you gain more knowledge in that area, you can be well positioned to perform usual activities in that environment, and it is important that your skills can be qualified through diplomas or other certifications that serve as proof of your professional career.

- **Define the type of work you want**

A common point of labor failure is that in the job search is not defined correctly the type of employment they want, to avoid this you must determine the type of people you are looking for or you plan to interact with, also if you know the schedule that most generates comfort becomes another objective when looking for a job.

In the middle of your expectations are also the benefits you are looking to get from your work, so you can start by creating a list with the section of requirement, preferred and non-core, so you can set your priorities on each aspect of the job.

Defining what you are looking for is what you should keep in mind in the middle of a job interview, because it is about your tastes, and what you do not consider fundamental to make a decision about a job offer.

- **Establish how your skills contribute to the job position.**

The job search estimates the economic benefits, compared to the personality traits you possess, since the contribution you want to show has a cost or an economic valuation, by identifying the characteristics of your way of being, you can quantify what you are worth to the company.

What is most valued in any job position and is recognized economically is punctuality, responsibility, commitment and capacity for group work, these must be presented on the assigned tasks, this becomes a brilliant performance that every business or company recognizes and seeks.

- **Identify the type of company you aspire to work in**

An important estimation before looking for a job is the place where you want to work, because the profile of the company should go hand in hand with your performance, this facilitates the adaptation and at the same time that you are satisfied with the space where you develop most of the day.

When faced with different employment options, you can evaluate the corporate culture, as well as the attitude of the managers and the organization it represents, you can study this based on what they offer you to generate an image of what that type of work will be like, this completely clarifies the option for which to choose.

What you should keep in mind about your professional profile

The formation of a professional profile helps you get the job position you expect, this is defined as a presentation face to a company or business, where some applicants have more experience in an area but this is not exposed correctly in the curriculum, making it difficult to find a job offer.

It is essential to organize every piece of information in your resume to clearly present your academic studies, knowledge, work experience, and also your aptitudes, in addition to the aesthetic side of including complementary studies, as well as your capacity in some objectives and areas.

- **Correctly state experience and training**

An important section within the resume is this one, where each education received and performed becomes experience, in the middle of this explanation you do not need to go into details, but you can mention the companies and the key functions you carried out, this allows you to design an attractive profile.

In the middle of this description you should place the work areas in which you have the greatest mastery, this allows you to clarify the strengths you possess, being useful to fulfill that particular job, in the middle of this explanation you can incorporate the command of languages and knowledge about certain tasks.

- **Frequently update your resume**

The presence of the curriculum must be taken care of at all costs, therefore the update is essential to add the courses and other training you are doing, that kind of information builds a solid professional profile, this also addresses the update of the design, so that it is adapted to the most modern format and is accepted.

- **The impact of photography**

An image is an aspect to place in the resume with a serious style, since it is an element that communicates a lot, it also works to humanize this professional presentation to give strength to the information in the text, it is recommended that you issue different shots or captures, without losing the sympathy and be a great impression.

- **Create an "about you" section to include details**

The section of the curriculum destined to your personality, should be taken seriously, because the characteristics should cause you to be seen or qualified as a suitable person to achieve the job you are looking for, in the middle of this section you can insert hobbies to clarify what you like the most.

These details are very useful so that at the moment of studying your professional profile, it expresses how you are on a personal level as well, in that way you can draw attention to other candidates' options.

- **Consult your review with another person**

Once you think your resume has been finalized, you may show it to someone else to note when a piece of information doesn't fit who you are or what you're looking to prove, or you may receive recommendations so that you can get great offers and have an ideal job.

Key actions to find a job

To test your personal offer in the work environment, you must be attentive to every environment that offers positions that fit what you are looking for, but in order to be in touch and not miss any opportunity, you must start by carrying out these actions:

1. **Post and comment that you are looking for employment**

The need to look for a job is not a fact that you should hide, but on the contrary, you should express your intention to obtain a job position or a change of employment, because this causes that the information can be expanded to find the available alternatives in the labor field, which allows you to select the best for you.

There is no doubt that you may come across job offers that you do not know in depth, it is a reality when you express your desires and the area in which you are interested, it is not about embarrassment, but to exploit some alternative, forming connections is important to identify some job availability.

2. **Register on some websites that offer job offers**

A frequent alternative nowadays, is to search and be part of online platforms that are specialized in this topic, since they are media where jobs are offered frequently, by doing this step you can expand the chances of receiving job offers, you can set notifications to always be aware.

In this kind of websites the value and the offer of your professional profile is taken into account, this is expressed through the information placed in digital forms, this is a way to make known the personal and academic details, these will be appreciated by companies and anyone interested.

3. **Make sure everything is correct**

On the professional profile it is very important that you can check that every detail is correct, verification is never too much, each piece of information must be presented in an ideal way, this includes not overlooking any spelling mistakes, much less that some representative element is missing.

4. Dedication for realistic job offers

Faced with some drastic situations, you may be desperate to get a job, but that should not be your motivation to act, because it can lead you to consider any offer that appears on the internet, or any call or offer, but you should be careful when presenting that rush.

Making decisions can lead you to be part of misleading jobs, or it may be a job offer that does not suit you personally, so after each job option you must visualize yourself in it, that helps to determine if it is a good offer for you, and also takes into account the economic factor and the type of company it is.

5. Keep an eye out for any contact

Answering or at least receiving a job offer quickly, helps to reaffirm your interest in that job position, this is often measured by the company, because if you are offered a job alternative, and you are slow to respond, that is interpreted as a sign of apathy so you must be fully attentive.

6. **Regularly study job offers**

The objective of getting a job is a constant work, you should not overlook any type of offer, on the other hand when you are part of a course or training you must modify your requirements, that is to say this implies that you are constantly updating what your skills offer, and the opportunities of the labor market.

Recommendations for starting a job search

The preparation of the job search is vital in terms of your personal presentation, so you must take care of every detail that is recorded in the curriculum, as well as what you are going to say in the interview, without forgetting that you must meet or have ready the general requirements that you may be asked to enter a job.

The usual questions to have access to a job opportunity, you can study them in advance, this allows you to have an assured way to expect or imagine what you are going to face, it is a way to reach a positive result on the job you are looking for.

In order not to overlook any type of offer, you can implement and follow the following recommendations:

- **Take care of your cover letter**

A cover letter is an ideal instrument to postulate your skills, this can be accompanied by a resume, this is a document that helps you to express other elements about your professional profile, you can clarify everything related to your knowledge and skills.

Extending what you offer at the labor level, is a reality through this document, where to expose the professional objective does not generate any problem, for this you can use different models of cover letters, where some can be used as a form of response to the announcement.

Another way to use it is as a spontaneous way to send your candidacy about your job offer, or it also works as a response to being referred by a family member or friend, without leaving aside that these documents are thoroughly read by a talent scout, so it is a way through which they can contact you.

- **Research resume templates**

The resume changes format every year or moment, for this reason when you decide to look for a job, you must ensure that you emit an appearance of an updated applicant, for this to include every piece of information that generates a great impression and at the same time that it is ordered correctly.

Normally the curriculum can be created with a basic approach, which you can find online and postulates a much more educational orientation, the development or narrative is presented through a chronological order, since ancient times this type of order is applied and is ideal for those seeking to stand out for academic merit.

Another style to use is the functional one, being one of those that imposes as protagonists the professional competences, in this way you can stand out for the type of functions that you are able to perform or that you have carried out, this does not have any type of chronological order and hides any academic deficiency.

A third alternative is under the combination of basic and functional style, being an appropriate way to describe both educational development and job competencies, this is used for applicants who have a high degree of experience showing off their educational background.

- **Improve the key points of a curriculum**

Having a responsible image when applying for a job is possible when your professional profile is valued. To make it easier for the hiring party to focus on these points, you should first of all ask yourself the following questions:

1. **Talk about you**

It is an important gap that opens within the resume, you must be careful with what you place in this space, because it is a means for you to describe those personal qualities and professional skills that allow you to stand out from other applicants, this should be aligned or focused with the type of position you are looking to reach.

2. **The reason why you are looking for a job**

The opinion you have about the job search is important for you to broaden your professional experience, this is a speech that you can put on your resume, because it is a way to highlight your positive aspects and shows that you are committed to work on this job.

3. **What do you know about the company?**

You must be careful about the consideration of the company, for that the best solution is to investigate thoroughly so that you can demonstrate that you are interested in being part of that organization, otherwise you can appeal to how much you like to carry out that job responsibility to frame it as a passion.

4. What is the highest priority in your life

This section means that in many resumes or interviews, it is answered that work is the most important thing in your life, which may be misplaced in many circumstances, and may even be assumed as false when, for example, it appears that you are married, so it is better to place and express that the essential is the improvement.

As long as you can define these kinds of impressions in a more friendly way, you can demonstrate that you bring value to the company, and at the same time seek well-being and comfort for yourself personally or as a family member.

5. The type of experience that corresponds to the job position.

When you find a job offer that is compatible with your professional profile, you should focus on the level of experience you have in that environment. If there is no compatibility, you can concentrate on increasing your skills and strengths so that you will be able to accept that type of position.

6. **What stands out about you professionally**

When you ask yourself this question, you should try that the answer goes in the same direction of the characteristics demanded by the job, since in this way you are more likely to find a positive response, for this it is always advisable that you define yourself as a leader, thus exposing your ability and ambition.

The ideal job search plan

When looking for a job you must keep in mind that it is a planned action, from the beginning you should try as much as possible not to neglect any aspect, so you must develop a plan to help you change your life, so you can use your skills to get where you want, performing these actions:

- **Explore your capabilities**

At first any job search can seem disorienting, but you can take control of it through your personal goals and the career profile you have established. For this to pay off, you must dedicate yourself to considering what you want to do and what you are capable of doing.

The coherence in pursuing and making these estimates a reality must be unique, therefore the professional objective must be located in the choice of how far you want to go, this can be measured based on a short term or long term, always with a direct vision of your interests and needs.

As you can inquire about this objective on a personal level, you can have greater initiative and clarity when seeking employment, as you measure any opportunity within the labor market with another type of more personal comparative, this in the end can guarantee you a greater permanence and that your role is scalable.

When you know what you want to do, you can become fully aware of who you are professionally, as well as demonstrate it on the job offer you have received, there is no doubt that it represents a key step.

- **Reflect and build a personal inventory**

To make a concentration of your abilities in front of some position, is a way to show your professional objective, this is an important mark to be more successful in the work environment, to help you you can build a scheme that exposes your professional profile.

In the midst of the personal definition, you can study the variables of your training, skills and competencies, in addition to the work experience you have in that environment, so that you can obtain full clarity on the type of activity you are looking to perform, until you reach the financial point and the working conditions.

You can not overlook the current market demand, you can add to this everything you think is relevant to your self-knowledge, the important thing is to take into account your preferences so that you are willing to fight and find what is most important to you, getting in touch with jobs accordingly.

The most demanded or exploited economic activities in your environment, are a clue on what you should focus on, because you can adjust towards those jobs to have access to opportunities, but to get there it is essential that you know the labor market.

• The functioning of the labor market

The labor environment can open many doors for you, but for that you must know the composition of it, which revolves around supply, intermediaries and demand, by defining each one you can get a vision of what you can find, in the case of supply it is about the jobs that are in the labor market.

On the other hand, the demand is made up of the people willing to fill this type of job offer. This point is very changeable nowadays, because it is a dynamic environment that requires updating the data or trends so that the personal offer is in tune with the available demand.

While within this environment, intermediaries participate, being entities that function to connect supply and demand, causing contacts to be made quickly and effectively, through technology this can be represented by means of different platforms.

A sector that has lost weight in the face of globalization is the public employment offer, being proposed by the public administration, but it is a reliable way due to the number of vacancies available, but there is a greater preference over the private sector because it is an alternative of higher remuneration in many cases.

These points allow you to structure a job search plan, without losing sight of the personal, social and labor reality, these three points merge to generate a perspective of the avenues you have available to reach a job you feel comfortable with.

It sets a trend the positive attitude that you can maintain about the job market, but above all recognize what you must expand yourself, this is dedicated towards knowledge, to be a suitable candidate for that job offer, so you can concentrate to go to the practice of job search.

- **The way to look for a job**

There are several options to look for a job, the most usual is under a network of contacts, since you only have to maintain active communication with friends, employers, and even training courses to not overlook the opportunity that is available, another measure is to respond to any type of job offer that has been published.

Another measure that allows you to be seen as a possible candidate is to apply through a self-candidacy, since you can offer your services to companies beyond being in search of a job, this can be used as bait to be considered at least.

Normally the decision on the resumes received depends on the database of candidates, friends and job boards, so self-presentation through these channels can help you get a job efficiently, so you should register the resume in some companies, and make full use of the virtues of social media.

You must think that the job search process is similar to the sale of a product, only in this case you are offering your services, so you must promote your characteristics, being a simple fact through personal analysis, and update your presentation tools.

- **The curriculum as a marketing tool**

The resume should not be seen or shaped in a boring way, you can rather adopt a marketing image, from the wording you can change the professional impression that you can perceive, this does not mean that it is necessary to lie or something like that, but that it is valuable information and above all that it is updated.

On the other hand, as it is an instrument that must attract attention, you must ensure that it is not long, much less forced, and it is not recommended that there is such an extensive focus on personal data, the essential is the professional field, where you can include qualities of value to be an attractive candidate.

The best thing is that for each application, you can adapt the resume to that search, so you can highlight some point that make them bet on you more easily, also do not need to include too much information, but the most relevant, always hand in hand with the type of application you're doing.

- **The most common types of resumes used when looking for employment**

At the classical level, a series of curricula are used that have marked the work environment, so you should know each of the following and choose the one that suits you best:

1. **Chronological**

In this case, the content of the curriculum can be ordered by dates, starting from the most recent to the most distant that has been developed in time, this is established especially for work experience.

2. **Functional**

This is an order that involves the training and experience that one possesses, this can be established in blocks so that the theme works as a classification of this data, this allows a person who has a striking training history to expose it with great lucidity.

3. **Europass**

It is a European type curriculum, which aims at a better presentation of skills and qualifications under a simple standard, that is of general use throughout Europe.

On the other hand, beyond the classics, there are curricula that have adopted a much more modern trend, in this sense, the following are used:

1. **Infographic**

When looking for a job, especially with companies that are in high demand, it is best to opt for a design that is simple and eye-catching, so you can receive more attention on the mountain of applications that exist, all thanks to reinforce the visual environment, opting for the power of infographics.

In some cases the applicants bet on the modality of the videocurriculum, being a presentation by means of videos, this can be used by means of an external hiring or by means of modern applications.

- **The relevance of a cover letter**

The accompaniment of the resume with a cover letter is striking, because you can use it as a business card, because you have the power to reflect and capture attitudes, skills and other aspects that you want to make notice, this can be done through a self-candidature because the company considers you more.

In any environment or labor market you wish to enter, the best thing to do is to build a cover letter so that you can take advantage of any vacancy that is available now or in the future.

How to apply by means of a self-candidature

When faced with the desire to work, it is important that you consider the initiative to present yourself to a company without taking into account whether it needs candidates or not, this is known as a spontaneous candidacy, over time it has become an effective strategy, because you do not face any competition and you can be taken into consideration in the future.

For this you must be prepared in advance, as well as be patient because that company may not yet have plans to make any upcoming hires, but these steps should preferably be taken in areas that you master so that you can stand out in the middle of the application.

Whether there is a recruitment advertisement or not, you can enter their database, or they will have knowledge of your skills for any need they may have, and the simple fact of visiting places to apply allows you to gain experience and knowledge in that field.

To carry out this type of job presentation, you can call by phone, visit the company in person, and other ways that you see as feasible, this means of job search can be useful in sectors such as hospitality and trade, likewise you can investigate the company to view the positions that you can find.

Measuring the opportunities of vacancies on a company saves you time and makes you not to be heavy at the time of issuing your presentation, but this is not an easy job, it requires commitment and a number of visits and research on companies, although it is usual to send it by e-mail, but it takes away your experience.

Self-employment

Applying for a personal business idea is also an alternative to exploit your professional skills, but for this you must study and overcome different conditions, although you must also have an established objective, professional profile and the market on which you want to work.

In this type of development, you must have full knowledge of the companies that operate in the sector, so that you can also generate income on that medium, this can be under the provision of running a business, or to independently exercise some kind of service based on your professional training.

But your own source of livelihood is concentrated entirely on your own actions, so self-employment is classified as a salaried job, where you can negotiate directly with customers, this can manifest itself as a sole proprietorship, since it is an organization made up of one person.

On the other hand, there is the way to carry this out with autonomy, where you do not belong to any company, but it is an offer of your services, and each of these forms of execution of self-employment allows you to have a life schedule tailored to your needs, without following any kind of guideline from an employer.

In the case of having your own company, you are much more inspired to make it grow into a large corporation, and the central point of these efforts is that you would be generating wealth for yourself, plus in your free time you can do other activities that you consider attractive to you.

But not all are advantages, because it implies a higher degree of responsibility and commitment, since you must personally cover the payment of taxes and any other management that represents the company, on the other hand must also carry out the payment of social security corresponding to the country.

Without leaving aside that the administration of a business is a considerable task, it is a path that requires self-discipline, and at some point it becomes addictive to disengage from the daily obligations to be faced, as well as the issue of income is variable, causing you to need an alternative plan for some periods of low production.

These risks can be kept in mind at the time of taking that big step, so you will be aware of what you earn, and the actions involved to reach that level, there is no doubt that it is attractive but requires adjusting to your professional profile, so you can exploit your professional capabilities.

Searching for a job on the Internet

In the Internet there are a lot of job offers, as well as ideas that you can use to your advantage, it is also a medium where you can present your resume, even to take advantage of some interviews that can be adopted by this way, all these aspects are essential for your development.

To carry out the job search by this means, is that you use the internet as your best ally, being able to study and bring out the main characteristics that are behind each job offer, so its main advantage is the universal side it has, to find a variety of published offers.

This medium is being used more and more frequently, thus a great diversity of web portals have been created that help to disseminate job offers, this is a more direct connection between jobs and applicants, at the same time this kind of website allows you to publish and share your resume.

Internet is a way to know better the companies and the labor market itself, this increases the possibility of being hired, without leaving aside that it is an effective means of research, reaching the sector in which you are most interested, this alternative helps you to be informed about any incidence of the labor market.

A way like the internet is a result of innovation, that is why it is classified as the channel with the largest job search, so you should take advantage of this alternative, which supports you to not have to waste too much time, now you should not leave home to know the offer of the labor market.

Before delving into all of the different aspects that are available on the Internet, you should know one basic point as follows:

- **Philosophy when looking for a job**

A key aspect to handle within the job search, is the attitude with which this task is carried out, because when you are issuing a wrong attitude, you will not get the results you are looking for, you must also take into account that looking for a job is a job itself, to the point of being an experience that becomes tiring.

This means that the more you focus on your preparation, the better the search process will be, so the main rule is to maintain a good attitude and predisposition, in each application it is essential to take care of discipline, so you can take advantage of the job opportunity that is ideal for you.

Regardless of the outcome that occurs, you should not get discouraged, beforehand you should not ignore that you will be subjected to various rejections, and this does not mean that you do not have to invest a considerable amount of time, the essential thing is that you can continue without decaying in the middle of the attempt, so you must follow your personal goals.

The thought to follow is that you take advantage of the time, through unemployment you must use that energy in favor, to put aside the obstacles, so do not take your eyes off your goal, that kind of momentum you can keep it by performing these activities:

1. **Volunteer work**

This kind of activity is useful so that your free time can be well spent, since you will be part of an occupation that raises your self-esteem, plus you can gain skills to be more useful, especially if it has to do with the field where you want to develop as a professional.

The time you can spend in the midst of these activities, makes you analyze if you are happy with what you do professionally, causing that in a negative scenario, you have the ability to open yourself to other paths or challenges, this can lead to take another kind of professional training.

2. **Specialization for being informed**

Above looking for a job, it is essential that you are informed of any details about the labor market, the same applies to the type of profession you perform, that way you will not miss anything new, taking advantage of this level of information so that you do not become rusty before modern knowledge.

This time can be used to take courses that you had postponed for so long, the ideal is that the time is spent in an effective way, this leaves an authentic preparation for the capabilities to be visible to the job search that is being performed.

Waiting for a job deserves a much more open attitude, because everything you are able to believe you can do, the positive attitude is very important above all, because if not all the effort is not worth much, it is advisable to present the best face and will to get to receive the job opportunity.

- **Motivation and positive attitude are key**

From the beginning of a job search, it is vital that you do not lose heart, much less confidence about yourself and what you are worth, you must convince yourself completely to be part of the opportunities available in the market, this spreads to others so that they see you as an ideal candidate for a position.

A positive mindset fades any obstacles to finding the desired job, as you are conveying that level of readiness to tackle any job offer, and that kind of attitude relates to a vision of success that can be used over a job sector to drive the dynamics of the environment.

Being in contact with clients and the interviewer with that kind of attitude is an advance itself, being able to combat any difficulties that arise in the midst of this job conquest, without seeing the options with a high level of hopelessness, is a way to get to get better results.

Beyond being positive, do not forget the proactive side to be eligible in the middle of the job offer, because it requires a greater ability to act without the need for your superior to ask for it, being a common hallmark nowadays, that level of encouragement is highly valued in jobs.

- **The importance of implementing self-esteem**

A healthy self-esteem is a push for you to present yourself in a more confident way to a job offer, makes it easier for you to keep a much more persevering attitude, that way you will get the job offer about the desired job you are looking for, in cases where you have lost the job you had, this is a start full of life.

Recognizing the usefulness that you have on some professional sector, also as a person, helps you to look for what you deserve, that is, you deserve it based on the training and experience you have, so it is valuable to have that kind of willingness to go further, thoughts in this direction help you get good news.

Little by little you can explore the work environment, without losing or damaging your self-esteem, no matter if there is a lack of response, because the job search process may be late, but that should not damage your intentions, as this can lead to a major depression.

Instead of throwing in the towel, you can only accept the rejection to continue looking for the desired job opportunity, without falling into sadness because it is only feeling is your worst enemy, in a recruitment are looking for candidates who have a high esteem, if you do not reach that level it is difficult to be hired.

• Means to search for jobs on the Internet

The first thing to exploit on the Internet are the means through which you can apply for a job, in turn it is essential to know how to use them so that you get out well on the labor level, so the main ways to take to progress at the labor level are as follows:

1. E-mail.

It is a direct means of communication on the Internet, you can take full advantage of the contact that the company has, it is a main way to communicate easily, to use this way to find a job opportunity, you must have an email account that emits a professional style.

In the middle of every communication you should keep a totally formal writing, you need to announce yourself with clarity and personalization on the name along with the surname, before sending any content it is vital to order each of the ideas you want to express, without extending, it is a brief communication.

By means of a simple structure you can succeed in this task, without forgetting that you need to take care of the capital letters, besides reading several times in order not to be shocking or aggressive, by means of being detailed you can give a great impression without creating predisposition on who reads it.

2. Google.

Online search engines are a comprehensive means to know what companies publish online, so no job offer can be overlooked, at the same time you can find websites that issue publications of being in search of personnel, so it can be used to reach job offers or companies.

This powerful tool is very useful, using it as it should, you can find and get lost in a large number of results when searching, but without losing sight of the value of the offers and real companies, there is no need to waste time, for that you have in favor of Google as one of the most important search engines.

The importance of this search engine lies in the way in which you can use it, so your main obsession must be to find the best results in Google, so that you get to the most relevant data, getting to that point is simple by placing "a position is offered for", or some "job offer".

You need to understand that Google establishes an index of what is written behind the content of that web portal, so when a company is looking for an employee this is filtered in Google in the way in which it expresses it, you must follow the usual type of words that are used to achieve this and have a better chance.

Use the first keywords when searching on Google that you can think of, as long as they are related to the job topic, you can look closely at each of the results displayed, and go through each of the websites, the main guide is the offer that appears in the main title, being useful in the future.

First of all you must choose the keywords, the more specific they are, the more options will emerge, in the same way you can restrict the results, by means of tools you can customize them to reach specific data, you can impose filters to facilitate the whole process, this is an excellent alternative for you.

3. Classified ads advertised online.

Job boards are available through the internet, because companies and prospective employees can connect seamlessly, it is an ideal environment to post jobs and have access to the job you want to achieve, these websites usually allow you to add data about yourself.

This option helps you have a direct way to get certified job offers, under a profile with or without experience, each portal seeks a competitive advantage for both parties, being a higher level of convenience, time savings and a greater possibility of searches.

Normally these website services are divided by section, on one side there are the applicants and on the other the candidates, having access you can consider some quotas, this freedom allows you to have the opportunity to classify the type of offers by activities and geographical areas through a registration.

Through these points you must include your resume, to consult every detail of the application, these online media are ideal for you to have a starting point to find the ideal job, using a large database, where they will view your resume a lot of job boards with great track record.

The job boards can be found by specialties, so you can filter by your area of greatest power the job offers that are available, the important thing is that it is a whole world available to offer you as a solid candidate, this is a margin full of opportunities.

4. Consultants.

A path after consulting firms, involves putting to compete or gain power through your resume, once you are able to upload this information you can take advantage of this formula that propels you towards high level job options, because if you prove to be attractive there is no doubt that a recruiter is going to contact you.

The increase of these possibilities can be manifested when you make a totally apt curriculum, in that way when it enters to some job exchange it will stand out, to make sure of it a consultant studies the presentation that you are emitting to the world, its operation resides behind the resources that are implemented to help the candidates.

E some alternatives the resume upload can be free of charge, but in most you must pay a fee for this push, as your proposal can be inserted into a database, in addition to passing reviews, you can opt for that bet so that the recruiter can be captivated by your data.

Once the resume goes through several tests, you can assume that the resume has keywords that should match the profile of the candidate they are looking for, because with an accurate description you have a lot to gain, but if you overlook these details they will not find you as a viable option.

Before you write and postulate your resume, there is no doubt that you should think about the type of words you are using, in the same way you should take care of the terms so that they are included on the radar of the company that is looking to hire, however over time the professional profile should also be updated.

These consulting companies are known as Temporary Employment Companies, where the advice to find the job you are looking for ends up being ideal, it is part of a resource for the future, but the fundamental thing is that they allow you to postulate the resume correctly.

5. Public employment.

Public jobs are posted daily on the Internet, this has to do with the classified ads that have been incorporated into technology, usually this happens a lot with jobs related to real estate, automotive and any other that has an online presence today.

Similarly, public jobs are associated with a modality or dynamic for life, different government institutions participate in this selection process, even the public administration has an impact, these are initiatives for citizens, even companies from their portals participate in this recruitment.

This way of looking for a job is very positive nowadays, they are environments that publish their job offers as a social contribution, in this media plays a key role the resume issue, you can visit these websites through Google, it is an option available for every need.

6. Social networks.

The relevance and impact of social networks on the job search is based on the number of people who prefer this medium, causing a large percentage to endorse this medium as the ideal one, making traditional media completely obsolete.

Most companies also keep looking for employees through this channel, and use it as a source of research to recognize candidates or applicants based on their profile on social networks or their portfolio, reaching a more serious job interview.

The presence in social networks is important for certain jobs, so it is best to keep them updated, as you can draw the attention of a company through this channel, this is part of that duty to sell yourself or apply a marketing that benefits you personally.

In the world social networks are used as a showcase to present your skills, you can also explain who you are and the ability you possess, so it allows you to convey much more than how empty a resume can be, the study of each social media leaves a glaring opportunity to seek employment successfully.

- **Recommendations when using social networks for job search**

One method of job search is the use of social networks, this is a valuable resource and can use each of its advantages, especially when it comes to a professional environment such as LinkedIn, or the use of Xing is also striking, but gradually Facebook has been useful for this mission, and this joins Twitter in the same way.

In each of the social points mentioned above, it is a duty to make close contact with companies where your profile fits, it is an active participation that allows you to connect with people or companies that interest you at the labor level, so the first duty you have is to design a list of contacts.

Establishing useful contacts in the environment in which you operate, helps to get a job, on the other hand the slope or main focus should not disappear from the profile, as it is a way to raise what interests you and thus you can build a concept of yourself, and the same goes for the company, because you will know what they are looking for in an employee.

This means that updating the profile is key, without leaving aside the care about the type of comments you make and the pictures you are sharing, for this you can have a professional profile and a more personal one, think about using and creating the following platforms:

- **LinkedIn**

It is a social network that has a professional network orientation, therefore its dynamics is to maintain full professional contact, the success within this network depends on the contacts and groups must be aligned at all times with the activities and interests of that labor sector.

This is a means to gain the attraction of companies and get them to consider your profile, so you must define objectives to implement on this social network, whether it is simply to seek employment or develop a business towards new customers, to get to connect with the leaders of the related industry.

The personal experience you have can be explained with the use of keywords, this implies paying attention to the certifications, profession and others, to comply with the profile data or update them as if it were a resume, without committing any spelling oversight, these details help to capture the attention of anyone.

A professional image can be easily conveyed through this channel, achieving to humanize the labor talents, it is a professional side that can be enhanced to the dynamics of this platform, in the case of LinkedIn, it has been frequently used to search for employment, being the true intention of its creation.

The experts in different subjects or headhunters, keep actively using this medium, so the main questions you should ask yourself is to define what you want them to see in your profile and if it is attractive to get to receive a job offer, by answering these questions you can move forward, also perform the following steps:

1. Configure LinkedIn properly, before using this social network you should study each function it provides, where you should be more careful is on the issue of

privacy, as you must select who can see the information you put about you.

2. Complete every detail of your profile, in the middle of the operation of this social network, you have the opportunity to use it as a digital resume, so it is a general rule to keep every piece of information current, this includes personal and professional details, so they can see and study your professional life.

3. Stand out from other users, it is key to broadcast the intention of finding a job, this can be included on your profile, without boring too much to the observers of this social network, but that headhunters can see what you are looking for or what they can offer you. Additionally you can use this social network to investigate a company, especially if it has to do with what you are looking for, so you can integrate it to your contacts, and so you will be the first to know if there is a vacancy that you can get, in this social network is much more beneficial to make friends.

4. Use keywords, this social network has a search engine where keywords have a great influence, as you can include the right ones, you can cause your profile

to be found more easily, to the point of coming across a good news.

5. Dedicate yourself to stand out within this social network, before any job offer that comes through this medium, do not hesitate to do everything possible to reach it, you should not wait longer than necessary to see the ad on the profile of the company or contact.

An option such as LinkedIn is classified as very valuable, because it is an environment where like-minded people meet, managing to form a professional group, this is highly useful when looking for a job, since it is a global network that builds contacts around your profession.

- **Xing**

The use of this platform is not attached to the functions that LinkedIn has, since it develops another type of modality to contact people, and has thematic groups to discuss and establish relationships in forums, thus generating a large number of job offers or publications of events of some companies.

The contact within this social network, is carried out through the contact request, which must be confirmed by the recipient, this allows you to create two-way relationships, the system itself helps each user to expose the profile information to attract attention.

Through the information that circulates in this media, weekly bulletins stand out, where you can find events, statistics and much more, you only need to complete the registration and the options are free, although there is a Premium user mode, which allows you to send messages to users that are not your contacts, for example.

To search for employment through this medium, you must carry out actions similar to those mentioned above with LinkedIn, although it is a social network with less reach than other social networks, but specialized in the creation of profiles to be found before a search for employees issued by a company.

With at least 45 million users, it provides an important level of visibility at the job level, being useful for business owners or any applicant, being a much more powerful or concentrated digital meeting point for that purpose.

• **Facebook**

Social networks such as Facebook have gained an important place to broadcast and obtain information, thus producing a much more optimal selection of personnel or employment, it is a medium on which more and more users resort to achieve the type of employment you had hoped for.

Just taking into account the number of users on Facebook, which exceeds 900 million users, obtaining a level of popularity as high as Google, it is a social network that works for recruiters, bringing any candidate closer to a job offer that is published.

The presence in social networks opens the doors to issue outstanding information to any company, it only takes a review of the profile to get an overview of the type of candidate you are, causing it to be a must to consider as attractive to sell your job skills.

The dedication on this social network shows a daily use of at least 20 minutes a day, this is an important data because it indicates that it is a considerable access point to find employment, but the care with the profile data increases, you can use to your advantage the amount of traffic that is on this social network.

From the Facebook profile you can measure many personal aspects, so you can not hesitate to present yourself as a very attractive future employee, the use of this medium to seek employment causes that certain standards must be met, where you can stand out as a reliable candidate and this goes hand in hand with what you post.

It is best not to criticize any company, no matter how well founded you are, much less to publish excessive photographs when you are looking for a job, because this creates an out-of-context presentation, and you will lose the interest of any recruiter.

In order to get a job offer within this social environment, you must take care to create an image suitable to attract the attention of a recruiter:

1. Provide a suitable profile picture, you should not take any risk for this small detail, since first impressions count, it is not necessary to exaggerate to create a presentation with work, but at least that does not go in telling the sector that you dedicate yourself.
2. Take care of every little description in the biography, descriptive details on Facebook need to be updated, this causes you to provide a better image of you, you can consult your profile with others to reach constructive criticism.
3. Include and add work experience data, it is essential that this kind of data cannot be overlooked, but without the need to expose all the details concerning your job description, you should only publish the personal and professional aspects that you want them to know.

4. Publish links to your portfolio or other sites, it is essential for them to measure your professional potential, building different professional profiles is a great help to position yourself in a better way, especially when you can include positive information about yourself.
5. Join groups on Facebook, in this social media there are several groups that are dedicated to the publication of job offers, so by becoming a member you can learn about the latest news so you can take advantage of these opportunities, and you can even interact with other applicants.

This exemplifies the type of tool that Facebook becomes to find employment, above all it depends on you, start considering this social network as something more than just social publications, so that the profile you build will get a much more professional value.

- **The role of Facebook groups and pages in finding jobs**

The main advantage of Facebook when looking for a job is that it allows you to locate contacts and share information, but the easiest way is to participate in topics within this network, where they are dedicated to finding employees and you can enlighten yourself with what is available by visiting a group that specializes in these publications.

A practical example of this is that you may be interested in a particular field, and to find related work on Facebook, you can add yourself to groups that are described as focused on that profession and the country you are part of.

This type of search can go from the most specific to finding groups that are really promising, each one retains a different type of orientation to find a candidate just about your preferences, to be part of this type of opportunities, you may have to request permissions to the administrator.

Normally you can be admitted if you comply with their rules of interaction, also a lot of groups are open, the difference between one and another, has to do with the preference of privacy, these environments impose the advantage of direct participation with other people and allows you to connect with your interests.

Another similar alternative is to communicate directly with the pages of the companies, since in Facebook different companies create these spaces to propitiate some interview, being a real interest that companies can manifest, and the user can contribute ideas or their skills to fit.

- **Twitter**

It is conceived as one of the most popular social networks, where job announcements are also posted, but it is used less frequently compared to the previous social networks mentioned, but it is important to be present and attentive to these incidences.

To look for work on this medium, you can implement the following suggestions that allow you to stand out in a simpler way:

1. Create a serious username, this allows you to gain a much more authentic presentation when looking for a job, it is a facility to widely use your profile as an eye-catching aspect.
2. It is a space that should be used in a broad way, because it helps to raise interest in your professional proposal, you can use the same when you know the intentions of a company, since it is a measure of visibility.
3. Set custom images, instead of using a default image, it is best to use your own design that allows you to identify yourself, especially taking into account that these details will appear in your biography, additionally you can take care of the inclusion of links.
4. You must tweet actively, it is important that when a company reviews your profile, it can find recent publications, in addition to having direct influence on information from the working environment.
5. Search for job offers, the search engine of this social network allows you to find a job posting, as recruiters can use this option to post a specialized opportunity.

On Twitter you can implement some tools to capture job opportunities, the essential thing is that in each social network you can open the door towards getting a job.

- **Google**

The development of Google as a tool for finding employment, has to do with the operation of Google Plus, where it uses that wide circle or level of data sharing, these utilities define important contacts, the essential thing is that you can form networks to find work.

Completing your profile in this tool allows you to let them know you until you get the job you need, but to do this you must establish the circles you want to see your messages, in the middle of that job search, you can add information about the job search you are doing.

In the middle of these functions is the possibility of adding company contacts, this demands that you must adapt the type of communication you share, because it is essential that the message can be exposed, it is common sense to use the medium in the best way to direct the best presence towards the companies.

A highlight within this social network is that you can position yourself as an expert, but reaching that level involves demonstrating that you know what you are talking about, you can rely on the use of Twitter, and other blogs to establish the type of opinion you have about that job sector.

Before this Google network, you should investigate the type of functions it currently has, because it can be an important point to exploit so that you get key results on the utilities that keeps creating this search engine.

- **Blogs**

An instrument such as a blog, becomes an ideal way to share your ideas, this works as a hook when you want to be noticed as a professional, it is a context to take into account because it postulates reasons for companies to decide to hire you.

Knowing about yourself is a key step for your interests to be a striking means to want to be part of any job, so if you do not have a personal blog, it's time to do it, because it is an invested time to be a candidate to be considered by the company that is hiring, it serves to present and future.

The main objective is that you have the freedom to express your interests and ideas, as long as they can be related to the labor field, this allows the job search can be better influenced, because when an employer can view your blog, they can have a much more dynamic image of your resume.

It is a must to write regularly, this allows visitors to find a blog much more nourished with information, as you can be more updated, you can get a degree of value that will appeal to any recruiter, but with the function of conveying a clear idea about your ability and job interest.

- **Objective on social networks**

The job search on the Internet is facilitated by the much more precise side because you can come across publications that express "looking for such a profession with experience in such and such", being offers that abound in this medium and are striking, allow you to adjust to the requirements to be considered as an applicant.

In the middle of this offer you can measure the type of employment that results, for this you must handle general data about the company, and to measure the work environment you can consult your contacts if any of them keeps working in that environment, being a concrete point to estimate the offer.

How to leverage the use of LinkedIn to search for jobs

There is no doubt that online, one of the best and largest professional networks is LinkedIn, as it is an ideal platform to reach an attractive job at national and international level, but you must know how to use it to make any goal you set yourself professionally a reality.

First of all, since its foundation in 2002, it has been dedicated to creating agreements so that it can develop a dynamic job market available online, where more than

200 countries can participate, in addition to large companies that use this medium to propose offers and find employees.

Recruitment is a measure that is easily developed in this environment, and works as a social network as it facilitates the issuance of information about the company, the publication of an event or similar action, so it is established as a tool used by most recruiters.

The operation is totally bilateral, to provide employment, as well as to search, this makes it a connection point not to be overlooked, but it is essential to use each of its functions to the fullest, where the first requirement rests on the creation of a solid profile, in addition to taking into account these details:

- **CV Online**

The ideal definition of LinkedIn is located as an online resume, by this means you can expose the data to be striking to companies, but it goes further because it allows the connection between each party to specify a job or position, so it is essential to ensure the creation of an appropriate profile.

The power of this kind of online resume, is that companies can have a direct access to your information, leaving aside the number of submissions of your resume, with a visit to your profile is enough.

- **Increases presence within this platform**

The job evolution that this social media provides is recognizable, it allows the aspiration to work can grow in a recognizable way, but it is not only about putting your resume out there, but you must be an active user, that way you can find some opportunity over a forum.

- **Customize the URL**

LinkedIn's own platform generates a URL when you create a profile, this can be edited to integrate your first and last name, it is a useful setting for the public profile can be a more striking description that you can include on another social network to drive traffic.

- **Establish that you are looking for a job**

In the middle of the job search, you can implement some keywords, this allows you to be found more easily when there is a job offer, this can be focused on the type of profession you have, which should be part of your profile.

- **Attracts attention with the profile**

There is no doubt that the LinkedIn profile must reach an attractive level, for this reason the keyword recommendations make sense, being a great identification, where the most important thing is that the professional experience can be highlighted.

- **Upgrade and increase your skills**

The presentation that you can create on your profile, should have a greater inclusion of skills, these should be attached or compatible with the area in which you work, this gives you unique advantages because they can contact you for how striking are your skills and the date of any additional training.

The summarized steps to search for employment in this medium is the registration or login, then there is the use of the search engine to find any job offer, where you can include the rada of using results from around the world, to be part of groups where all kinds of jobs are offered and should not stop working on the network and number of contacts.

Tips for finding a job

When looking for a job, it is worth focusing on the available options, instead of concentrating on the refusals you receive in the middle of this search, because what acquires greater value is the insistence at the moment of finding an opportunity.

1. **Investigate zonal options**

Around your environment or locality, you can find businesses that keep publishing the application for a job, so go through the most adjacent areas, can lead you to the options you need, this is usual in businesses related to restaurants, it is a way to take advantage of the free time you have.

Faced with a complicated situation, this is an ideal solution, because it helps you to stabilize yourself at the labor level, and then move on to other alternatives. It is important not to discard this type of path, since it places you in front of a totally valid work option, depending on the situation, but it can be a reasonable path.

2. **Visit and explore employment websites**

A very used option nowadays is the bet on websites that are dedicated to the job search, they are portals that contain a variety of offers, where you can find the type of alternatives that exist in your sector, until you come across local offers, as well as international as a remote development.

For each region there are portals with greater power, it is simple in Google you can find a whole panorama of options for your location or for the profession you are performing, so it is a positive scenario for you to save time and headaches, as it is a more direct way to find employment.

3. **Betting on employment agencies**

A modern technique that facilitates all the paths to a job, and at the same time can prepare you better, are the employment agencies that can be established directly on your location or with an online management also works, even the States have taken charge of participating in these initiatives.

To link with a decent job offer compatible with your ambitions, you can explore this path, where the main performance is based on the active way of communicating that you are looking for a job, including the recognition and advice provided by these services with international reach.

4. Leveraging professional social networks

The use of Facebook, LinkedIn and others such as Xing or Viadeo, work as an advertisement of interest of wanting to get a job, for this to become a reality it is essential to form a real profile that is representative, you must keep in mind that you need to sell yourself as an authentic professional.

On the other hand, this kind of social environments should encourage you to generate future work relationships, the secret of everything lies in the type of relationship you are able to create, so you can receive job offers or on the other hand, you can send your resume to tempt a company, being useful when your skills back you up.

5. Take advantage of the networking network

Implementing networking as a means to create interpersonal relationships, helps you to obtain a base of useful contacts, being a wide path to all kinds of opportunities, all thanks to a social effort on your contacts so that those relationships serve as an impulse to reach job or business offers.

Through professional contacts, you can sow a high degree of affinity, which can translate into a direct benefit for you, so the sooner you start, the better the results will be until it is much more spontaneous, in the case of having them, you must resort to them to obtain employment.

6. **Sending resumes to companies**

This technique is daring because you expose yourself to a greater amount of rejection, but sometimes you may be surprised by the results, just select the type of company you want to work for or the ones that best fit your skills, and contact the human resources person to issue your resume.

Normally you can send a letter, as a much more pleasant requirement, the essential thing is that there is a compatibility with your training and the type of company in question, that way they can see some direct benefit on the alternative of hiring you, leaving aside that cold treatment that can increase your chances.

Finding a job abroad without suffering in the process

Before a trip or an opportunity to live in another country, it is a great need to recognize the way to look for job options, that level of experience deserves to take into account some keys to not fail in the process, so to reach that goal in another country, you can follow some useful tips and great results.

- **Select the destination and find out about every detail**

A great trip can be assured and starts from the information you have, so before making any decision it is essential that you know the country thoroughly, on the internet you can find the material you need to take this step more safely, it is essential that you describe the destination before moving.

This is compatible with the idea of choosing a country that is compatible with the professional profile you have, as well as being close to the tastes and possibilities of the environment, but you should not overlook the level of growth or salary it provides, in addition to the burden of public services.

- **Identify the type of professional experience available to you**

Having chosen or imagined the type of professional experience you have, you can go on to consider certain steps to decide, including the type of life you wish to lead abroad, as well as establishing a financial plan to know if you intend to work seasonally and prioritize the vacation aspect.

On the other hand, you can keep in mind the path of working and studying at the same time, to continue acquiring more professional skills, through these questions you can set certain goals at the time of making a trip, where you can not overlook that enriching contact that involves being in another country.

- **Prepare your academic documents**

Beyond making some basic decisions, the next thing to do is to have ready the documents that will allow you to look for and get a job abroad, the most important thing is the type of degree, you must present the most recent one, in addition to being adapted to international legislation so that there are no problems and it will be accepted.

On the other hand, you can present diplomas that accredit the work skills that you have, in this way you add yourself to be part of those interested in some position, but these rules are different for each country, so do not hesitate to submit your proof of professionalism to a validation that generates freedom for you.

- **Increases language proficiency**

Finding a job beyond qualifications and job skills is not enough because you must go further and take care of the communication issue, so you need to master the language, but it is not enough just to be bilingual, but go further to trilingual and have an international certificate that can confirm it.

In a country that imposes an advanced command of the language, you will not suffer any limitation, much less for you to carry out your profession, so as a foreign worker you need to master these details, to be a local yourself, also this facilitates any application for visas or other immigration procedures.

- **Adapt the format of the curriculum to the country of destination.**

When looking for a job abroad, it is of great relevance to have a resume that is attractive by itself, without leaving aside that classic style of formality and elegance, this should not be any obstacle nor is it complex, you just need to work on it.

The first step is to find out how to make a resume for that country you have in mind or for that continent, so with basic concepts you can start writing it, but not only the content is important but also the structure, since the whole style must be estimated towards the country of destination.

- **Become part of online job boards**

Once you have a resume that goes hand in hand with the requirements of the country of destination, in addition to having the language certificate, it is time to look for the job you want in another country, this process can be developed from your computer to be part of job boards or a website of that country.

At the international level you can find some response from some portals, these impose a job offer globally, such as Indeed's function shines and another option of Freelancer, as this allows you to search in Google some available website about that country you are targeting.

Find a job in digital marketing

Finding a job opportunity in the digital marketing environment can be complicated, especially because as a beginner you may see your aspirations at a lower level, compared to the intervention of agencies, consulting firms, startups, and other businesses located on this sector.

Entering into this dynamic may seem impossible, but from the first day you can work for it, to reach a minimum opportunity as an intern or junior within an advertising agency, to reach these results you can explore all the alternatives that exist for you to integrate into this development.

1. **Build a digital presence**

A priority step, at the same level of the curriculum is the care of the digital presence, since when researching an online alternative or discovering a job offer, what they will evaluate is the type of image that you present in the social media, so a fundamental step is to form a professional profile on Instagram and Facebook.

In every online corner you can approach towards an offer, once you have created a solid professional online presentation, causing a call for attention on human resources personnel, so ask what you want them to see from you, and what will make you stand out and get you hired.

At the same time, you can participate in blogs, create podcasts or present some certificate that you possess, that way you can issue a hook to try to capture the interest of others, you are going to get a position or a much more special position than the others, being a point to stand out as far as digital marketing is concerned.

2. Education

Having the opportunity or access to these positions in digital marketing depends on the level of study, this demands that behind your presentation there may be a reputable university that supports the source of origin of your knowledge, it can be a bachelor's degree or a master's degree as a specialization.

This type of path or presentation is one of the most decisive, because if you have professional skills in advertising, economics or public relations being very related to what is needed to manage marketing activities, but some other parallel specialization can help you to get noticed more easily.

3. Internships or work experience

In the world of advertising, it is very important to incorporate practices especially to impose yourself more useful in the medium of communication or digital marketing itself, regardless of whether you have started in a large or small company, the essential thing is that they are solid first steps on a topic of interest striking.

The advantage of internships is that they can be used as a point of contact with the reception of job offers, using that learned knowledge or the name of the company as a presentation itself, normally a minimum period of stay of 6 months should be established on those positions to use them as a reference.

4. **Define where to look for digital marketing jobs**

To find jobs related to digital marketing, you can bet on LinkedIn, and others, as these are portals dedicated to that you can assess a digital job offer, under this same style also highlights We Are Hiring being one of the pioneering portals for this purpose in Spain.

Another platform to search for jobs on this category is Bebee, as it frequently focuses on the digital marketing theme, along with the operation of Ticjob being a portal also very important to get jobs, although it maintains a focus on IT professional actions.

5. **Sites where you can present your desire to work**

The action of looking for work specializing in digital marketing, is not only about sending resumes, but it requires vision, as this allows you to recognize what you want to be in the future or where you can develop, that kind of quality will cause that they can be exploited to the fullest.

You should not only limit yourself to getting it right, but it is vital to know much more, so that social networks are employed to the fullest as an essential communication to recognize the options available, being a professional measure to choose a better way to stand out either as experts on Pinterest or Instagram.

6. **The curriculum**

A determining aspect is to maintain an impeccable digital image, without leaving aside the intention of learning all the time, without any intention of stagnating, this allows you to reap interest, and the same happens with your profile, it must be a point of attraction itself, without forgetting the constant updating.

There are many alternatives to take care of and improve your resume, if possible you should invest for being a marketing specialist, as this helps you to stand out over the offers that exist within this field, fitting over profiles such as SEO, SEM, Social Media and others.

Finding a job without experience

In any circumstance, the job search without experience can be a headache for any applicant, since you must overcome the common requirement of having verifiable mastery of some field, this may seem impossible, but the solution lies in the willingness to achieve a higher level of knowledge.

The leap and the great action of boosting your personal presentation, is a duty that you possess with yourself, that way you can set aside those offers that are low in salary, so you must compensate the offer of your skills to reach other figures, so the way forward is the following to find employment:

- **Form a résumé or cover letter**

The development of the resume of an applicant with little experience, is often poorly ordered, since a lot of irrelevant information is placed, as many bet on trying to present a longer resume, but this is considered a mistake, since it is best to conduct a market study.

Once you can figure out what direction to aim for, you can present a more relevant type of information, because the job sector is what tells you what type of training is in demand, as well as the skills to meet the objectives of that field, which helps shape your resume by highlighting these details.

- **Submit your job application in the indicated media**

Once you have created the resume with the above-mentioned indications, the next step is to apply for the corresponding position, but in the middle of this process you should avoid sending a massive resume to any kind of company, do not get carried away by anxiety, it is advisable to consider the job position beforehand.

When you receive a job offer, what is measured is the type of skills you possess, as these need to be compatible, since the entire proposal must go hand in hand with the training you have, so that the job is taken advantage of in a comprehensive manner.

- **Increase your skills and demonstrate successes**

At the moment of being in full job search, the first step is to cover the introspection, for being a help to delimit the aptitudes as well as the achievements, in that way they are transformed into outstanding data on the curriculum, being an ideal letter to highlight in an interview.

It is often overlooked, but a training or internship experience abroad is an ideal way to be a much more relevant candidate. To recruiters, this type of experience is unique because it provides a greater amount of feedback about your company and is profitable for your organization.

- **Demonstrates a willingness to acquire more knowledge**

A recruiter takes into account the willingness you have to incorporate more knowledge, that kind of learning is a striking factor, since it is a level of interest that a job needs and by including that premise you can get hired, to exploit that desire for professional improvement.

- **Training is the main way**

Being without any work experience, training is one of the most treasured points when applying for a job and investing for it is of great help, so a key step can be the acquisition of more knowledge, this must be demonstrated on your resume to take advantage of it as a hook to the recruiter.

In order to fulfill that striking side of training, you can opt for free courses, that way you can enhance your skills, the agreements that companies make with universities, are a point to estimate to reach an attractive level of training, they are steps that bring you closer to a better professional quality.

- **Retains an active participation**

In such a competitive job market, it is complicated to establish a job offer search, so you need to keep a much more active attitude to capture the available vacancies, it is advisable to establish some alerts from websites, as this allows you to know about any job vacancy.

In the midst of this process, you need to remain patient, beyond any response it is vital that you do not get frustrated by the results, in the short term you may not meet your expectations, but over time persistence will lead you to a better work stay.

The best job portals

Job portals are an exclusive way to come across an important number of job offers, they maintain a dynamic labor market and help you get a knowledge of what is available for work, where the best ones to carry out your professional goals are the following:

1. **InfoJobs**

It is considered as a highly effective job search platform, since it provides a great amount of options, you can search in a personalized way through the companies or go to a category research and even design alerts so that you do not miss anything new.

In addition, when you select a particular sector, you can get high level advice for you to study what is related to this medium, so that any doubts can be dispelled until you get a better presentation.

2. **Monster**

This platform allows you to reach a large number of offers, since it publishes jobs both nationally and internationally, among its functions is the use of an advanced filter, with the possibility of uploading your resume to receive guidance regarding your training and aspirations.

3. **I want a job**

A search engine of this type, focused directly on the Chambers of Commerce, you must register to use this way, so you will have the opportunity to apply to any job offer, without leaving aside that it facilitates the improvement of your skills to increase training and have a network of contacts.

4. **Infoempleo**

A portal that leads the active job search is this one, since it has the same operation or dynamics as InfoJobs, the capacity of this search engine lies on the offers it provides where news and advice are issued to make professional training an attraction.

5. **Eures**

It is considered a European website, through which you can obtain offers and information related to professional mobility, it is ideal for anyone who wants to work in a country that is part of the European Union, so it is a portal of great relevance for you to cover your preferences and follow the procedures outlined.

Tips for finding a job when you are over 50 years old

Before any unemployment crisis, it is essential to get a job again, beyond being 50 years old, or at least consider offers to occupy your mind and use your skills to continue producing income, age is not a limiting factor nowadays, much less because of the power of technology.

The imbalances of the economy as a global fact of the size of Covid-19, emit a great motivation to seek some opportunity and overcome the ravages of these situations, where the experience should not be wasted but on the contrary, self-esteem should be at the top, to use that knowledge as a point of attraction.

The solution may lie in participation in volunteer work, so that the level of usefulness can be considered as a value itself, where discernment is used to help those who have no clarity about future decisions, that level of support is profitable in society and in confusing situations.

What is required to take advantage of job opportunities regardless of age are the following tips:

- **Be compassionate and highlight your skills**

A primary tip is to emphasize confidence in your abilities, as the job search is a scenario that demoralizes anyone, but the essential thing is that you do not weaken in the face of the responses you reap, beyond rejection, the vital thing is to take everything calmly, and when a stumble occurs, you can move on.

- **Discover your strengths and experiences**

As a candidate, it is essential that you are aware of what you are worth to face any job opportunity, so that the search for job offers can be carried out with greater success and discernment, that is easily reflected with keywords that are included on your resume.

Insert your qualities is a striking aspect in social networks, as this can be valued to obtain some position by a company as remote tasks, this means of action is simpler in every way, it is easily executed through platforms or job portals.

- **Willingness to change professional sector**

In some sectors of great concurrence, the most recommendable thing is to have in mind to go for a different industry, this is a key step that when having it key you can put much more of your part to obtain the job you are looking for, when knowing where to go and what you are willing to do, the way is facilitated.

The training and technology necessary to take that step, is a support that allows you to achieve daring to take a definitive step towards a comfortable job, so modern trends are a starting point on which to adapt, age is only a sign of experience, this you can use it to your advantage, as long as you accept modern utilities.

www.ingramcontent.com/pod-product-compliance
Lightning Source LLC
Chambersburg PA
CBHW070435220526
45466CB00004B/1680